be

YOU

...on

PURPOSE

DeLana Rutherford

be

YOU

...on

PURPOSE

Marquis Boone Enterprises
NewYork *Atlanta * Baltimore

MBE books may be ordered through booksellers or by visiting www.marquisboone.com

Because of the nature of the Internet, any web address or links contained in this book may have changed since publication and may no longer be valid. The views expressed in this work are solely those of the author and do not necessarily reflect the views of the publisher, and the publisher herby disclaims any responsibility for them.

ISBN: 978-0-692-41670-9

Printed in the United States of America

MBE Publishing rev. date: 04/15/2015

Dedication

This book is dedicated first to God, my family, Myles, Brooklyn and Lyncoln for standing with me, believing in my dreams and vision and never doubting what was in my heart. Then, I would like to dedicate it to all of the brave souls in this book who chose so willingly to pen their stories to bless so many others. In a world where so many pretend to be ok and never share their story, these people were brave enough to share theirs on another's behalf. Each one of these stories have impacted my life in some way. I know each of these people personally and I count it an honor to have them be a part of this be YOU on purpose movement. Thank you for being so real and opening up about so many things that have caused you pain and so much more. I know this book will touch many lives because of your sacrifice.

Thank you!

MY STORY

Can't catch my breath! Full of insecurity, anger, anxiety and fear!

It started as a teenage girl...

I was 15, getting in fights, heart racing on my way to class, full of anxiety and didn't know why. I'm a Preachers Kid, but at times I felt like I was going to die.

So many people put unnecessary pressures on me growing up. I remember when I was 9 years old, my Sunday School teacher announced in class that I was to be everyone's example in my class and have my Bible with me. It started so young and so many people didn't even realize what they were doing to a little girl that just wanted to be NORMAL.

My parents were amazing and very involved in leading me and my 2 older brothers in the right direction, but both of my brothers discovered and fell in love with drugs early in their teen years. All types, any kind. This began to take a lot of my teenage years away from me because my parents had so much focus on my brothers and ministry and simply trying to survive. Survive mean church folk, religious know-it-alls, finances, stress and so much more. So many Sunday's, I was told to put a smile on my face and walk in the sanctuary like nothing was wrong. I watched my parents do this week after week while we were all hurting so deep. Everyone expected you to be there for them, but who was there for us?

I remember being 15 years old, sitting in class one day and everything went blurry, or many other days when I was so weak and full of anxiety that I couldn't breathe. My teacher would send me across the hallway in a closet to catch up because I was so behind due to the stress in my life at such a young age. I would pick fights almost weekly because I had so much anger built up. I was angry at my brothers, angry at church folk because they would turn and leave my parents when they were in so much pain...Just angry!

My love for God was deep and my convictions strong, but it was my sophomore year that I said, "I'm going to numb some of this pain I'm in too". I began to go out with one of my brothers and he would only let me drink if I was with him, so I did. It would feel good for a little while, but the conviction was too strong to keep it up. Every week, in the midst of me going through all of this, I would go to the ball park in between services on Sunday and would line the pews up with guys and girls that needed God. I would preach to them with no compromise and watch each one come to the altar by the end of each service. One of my dear friends' mother, Marijo, whom I still love and talk to, called me and asked me to start traveling to school assemblies with her and the Crisis Pregnancy Center to sing and speak on Secondary Virginity. I was honored, but still afraid. I said yes because it fulfilled me to help others! Even though I knew I could sing, I was so shy when it came to the stage. My first solo was when I was 9 and I didn't solo again until I was almost 18 in a talent show.

Fast forward...

I'm 18, graduating (barely) only by the grace of God and Mrs. McNally, my favorite teacher and support away from home. She would push me every day while also telling me, "I see your stress...Lay your head down on your desk." I was in a relationship that was going nowhere. I'll never forget the day I had enough. At the time, my brother had cleaned up and was in Bible College and said, "I'm coming home to get you". I agreed and went. It wasn't but a few days until I met the man beyond my dreams and fell in love instantly! He sang, was good looking and crazy about God! We went through a lot to get together and although I wasn't too used to chasing any guy, I chased him for 4 months, gladly. I've always been the type to go for what I want and don't stop until it's mine. Finally, he moved to Tennessee where my family pastored. We dated six months and got married six months later. He worked under the leadership of my parents for almost 12 years. We worked with the Music team, Outreach, Youth, Dance, Elders and anything else we could get our hands in. We lived in low income housing and did whatever we had to do before we became full time in ministry. We were consumed! We had our beautiful daughter, Brooklyn in 1998 and our handsome son, Lyncoln in 2001. He was born 8 weeks early, only three pounds and six ounces. They told us they didn't know if he was going to survive. I never have liked no for an answer. He made it and our family was now complete.

I will never forget the day Myles looked at me and said, I believe God wants us to Pastor full-time. I looked at him as if he had lost his mind. I told him we could buy a bus and travel the world and sing for God, but there was no way possible that I would be a senior pastor with him after all I had seen my parents go through! Even though I knew it was wrong and not very submissive, I told him God would have to speak to me directly for me to make that move and commitment. It was only a few months later that I said yes. I will never forget my mother calling me and saying, "DeLana, I would love to tell you to put on your shoes and run", and as she began to weep she said, "But you would never get away from this calling". She began to encourage me and tell me I could do this and I believed her. She was my best friend, mentor and my mother and all I could think of was how am I going to leave her and my father and all I have ever known for over 30 years. My identity was once again being taken from me.

We begin to pack everything up, sold our home and took one year off to be with my husband's parents before we started this new journey. I'll never forget sitting in the grass in my in-laws back yard that night once we arrived and crying my eyes out asking God to please lead us and help us know what to do next. I was so afraid to leave what I had always known. We served in a church there for exactly one year before we moved to Kennesaw, Ga. We sold almost all we had, packed the U-hauls, our 2 young children and left every bit of family and all that was familiar to us to a city that seemed so overwhelming. We started our church, Worship with Wonders in a movie theater and stayed there for 9 months. We would take a trailer and set up and tear down every Sunday. We finally found a cave that was a dump at the time. We moved in after many miracles to be able to afford this 27,000 square foot building that was not a pretty site. We went through makeovers, let downs, sewage floods, long days and nights and much more with only about 30 people at the time. One night we were lying in bed in our little 2 bedroom apartment. Our kids shared a bunk bed and were sleeping. We heard someone banging on the door, yelling, "Get out!! Fire"! We scooped both kids up in a blanket and ran outside. I remember sitting in our car and calling my parents at 3:00 in the morning crying and saying what have we done. I just want to come back home! Although the church was growing, we were weary.

It wasn't long after that, I was in a service and I was doing what I love the most, worshipping and working in the altar. I laid hands on just about everyone there. A few of the ladies walked me back to my office and I asked them to leave me there to spend some time with God. I began to cry and before I knew it, I was going through deliverance. All of the rejection and anger was leaving me. I didn't even know I had so much. That following Wednesday night I didn't feel good so I stayed home. I was sitting on the couch alone and I had a visit from Satan. I had never experienced anything like this before. He said, "If you will leave the people alone, I will leave you alone". Now, I was a fighter growing up and I hated when people threatened me. I've always loved seeing people delivered, but this time, I was paralyzed. I couldn't speak or move. The same time this was happening, they were driving my husband home from service early because he had a physical attack in the pulpit. We had a few prayer warriors come in the house and begin to pray. Our daughter, Brooklyn was about eleven at the time and she said, "I feel death in here." My husband got up and begin to play the piano and I began to speak in my heavenly language until we felt some peace. We knew at this time that we were beginning to take territory and the enemy hated it! Little did I know, the most hell I had ever been through was about to begin.

Days later, I started a few medications for a sinus infection and I was home alone. I began to shake all over and felt as if I was about to die. I called my husband on one phone and 911 on my cell. All I could do was speak in tongues. I remember laying on the floor and thinking these are my last breaths. I won't even get to say goodbye to my family. Over the next 3 months I ended up in the ER many times with adrenal exhaustion. My parents came to pick me up for a weekend because my husband couldn't leave the church on a Sunday. When they arrived, I had dropped to 97 pounds and had no desire to eat, talk or live. They took me home to Tennessee and one morning while they were all laughing downstairs having breakfast, I walked down the stairs and yelled, "someone get me some help! I can't breathe and I'm losing my mind!"

My mom called her Natural Doctor and he's the one who discovered the adrenal exhaustion. He told me I couldn't do anything for the next 8 weeks to get them a jump start. No meetings, no caffeine, no sugar, hardly anything. I went home and this continued for months. I was so depressed. I had no desire to get dressed, go anywhere or even speak. I was sitting in my bathroom one day looking out of the window into our back yard and said, "God, if you are not going to heal me, please take me and let my family be happy." I felt so disconnected from life and everyone around me. It was as if I was there, but I wasn't there. I was miserable! My faith was questioned, my love for church, God, everything was unstable. At this time, I also discovered that I had a hormone imbalance which is also effected due to adrenals being depleted. Even though I was numb, I knew I had to cry out to God in my silence. There was an inner cry for help that I held on to everyday. Myles would look at me daily and say, "You are going to be ok." I believed him somehow and would wait for those words every day. I had waves of my heart racing, thoughts uncontrolled and wanting to die, but I knew I had to push through this and make it. I was standing on the stage on Easter Sunday, 97 pounds and very fragile mentally, physically and spiritually, and I began to lead worship and chills went through my whole body. I felt His presence again and began to cry because I knew then, the God I loved since I was a little girl, was still as real to me then as He was all along. Slowly but surely, I was healing spiritually and naturally. This came with many sleepless nights, major health changes and choosing my battles.

I learned so much during this time of my life. I had let life, ministry, people and so much more take from me and had gone my last mile before my body and mind began to shut down. Although a lot of this was natural things I had to change, I also know the enemy tried to use it against me too. He came at my weakest time and tried to take me out. It was not long after all of this, God began to send so many people to our ministry that had depression. Now, not only could I sympathize with them, but I could empathize as well. God has used me so many times to free people from depression since then. I am forever grateful that I didn't waste that dreadful season of my life, but chose to learn from it and use it for His Glory.

We are faced with so many things in life and we have to make the choice if it will take us out or we will overcome. When we go through things, it's always about helping others when we come through. Being a Pastors' daughter and a Co-Pastor along with all of the other roles we as women play, is not easy, but is very rewarding when we stop to count our blessings.

After I was healed inside and out from this, as I was leading worship, I would always say be YOU on purpose to the congregation. One of our members came to me and said, "Pastor D, can we please make this t-shirt?" Of course I said, yes. I didn't even realize I had said it that much, but I was really trying to live it myself. For years, I had been everything everyone else thought I should be. I started getting this for myself and I started finding the real me. Finally, my true identity was coming forth and I was liking it. I was finding happiness in being me and learning the real me was really a good person and it was ok to be loved and cherished for just that. I love to give to others and believe in them so I decided to make this a movement. I wanted to hear everyone's story and celebrate them. We made the t-shirt, we started a women and girls' conference experience and it was a huge success! I always loved fashion and decorating and desired to have my own store. I dreamt about that for almost 10 years. Finally, one day Myles and I were walking through a little town called Woodstock, GA and he said, "Do it DeLana! Let's open your store here." I had seen God do so many things for us through the years, like our son making it after 3lbs, our home that we believed for over 18 months that was a foreclosure on 5 acres that was my dream home coming true, cars he had given us, my mom being healed of MS and Breast Cancer, our church building and so much more. So why not? We were opening the first be YOU on purpose Boutique within one month of this conversation. God came through once again. They said they didn't have anything available for 5 years and within one weekend, someone wanted to move to another state and we took her place. God is always faithful! We opened September of 2013 and God has used that place for His Glory over and over. We accept prayer requests, the walls have others' testimonies and people stand and cry reading them as they receive hope. We support over 12 missions from different companies we buy from and so much more. It truly is a shop with a purpose experience. I am doing what I love and being fulfilled every day.

We have had teenagers live with us to help them get a start on life, we give weekly and it's true, it's better to give than to receive. That always comes anyway. The best thing you can do to help yourself is to find someone else in need and begin to help them find their way. I stand amazed every year of our women and girls' experience to watch layers fall off of them and years of pain being released in such a nonjudgmental atmosphere. People are hurting and we can't ignore it.

There's so much more to my story, but you get the point. I went through a lot of hell, misjudgment, unnecessary expectations and a lot of approval performances that God never asked me to perform. I'm thankful for every lesson, my heritage that sustained me, my family who pushed me, and for a God who is forever faithful.

Don't let others drain you and always make sure you are in the right place for replenishment. Invest in you or you are no good for anyone else. Breathe and be YOU on purpose.

"If He did it for me,
He can do it for you… Anything is
possible!"

DeLana Rutherford

I had a tremendous lack of confidence.

Even though I was celebrated all my life growing up because I could sing and I was charismatic... Yes something inside of me kept telling me that even though everybody else believed in me, I couldn't believe in myself. My confidence level hit rock bottom in college when people that I looked up to greatly wouldn't recognize me. I ended up thinking to myself I've got to be like this person or that person in order to be successful in ministry. I can truly say that I was trying to be everybody else and imitate what I thought the anointing was. I remember standing in my bedroom during the younger years of our marriage telling my wife that even though we were ministers, I feel like I am doing things in ministry to make everyone else happy... I remember saying, if this is Pentecost, I don't want it! But the truth is it wasn't Pentecost...it was me trying to emulate others' version of Pentecost. I was frustrated... I had lost my confidence trying to be what I saw others trying to be. It was at that point that I begin to find myself.

My wife's slogan has meant the world to me! The simple saying..."be YOU on purpose" has been a part of the important process of freeing me to BE ME. Finding my lane in life and understanding that even if I don't fit circles or look like others, I am simply satisfied with who I AM! The hardest person in life to believe in is ourselves, simply because we know everything about that person. Now I truly celebrate the God in me and I am in full confidence knowing that what He has for me... is for ME! I am confident in this one thing... "He who began a good work in ME is faithful to complete it!"

- Pastor Myles

"Just because people don't appreciate your love/giving, don't stop. It's who you are & what fulfills you."

DeLana Rutherford

I've been a Pastor's kid since I was about 7 or 8

years old. There's a lot of advantages and disadvantages to that. I grew up very stable and I'm forever thankful for such a strong and God-fearing family. I was taught to always treat others how you would want to be treated. I was the type of person with a huge heart... Definitely get that from my parents! However, I've learned that having a big heart could be used against me by others. So many times I would get close to the very same ones that would hurt me in the end. I never could've imagined treating people how they treated me. I felt as if I would drop everything to be there for someone but they would just use me when they had no one else at the time. I was very quiet and laid back, never wanted to cause any division. I started becoming insecure and trying to find approval from others around me. I was so caught up in what people thought of me. Being the Pastors daughter is a lot more pressure than anyone can imagine. Sometimes I felt that I couldn't do certain things that others could just because of the pedestal I was on. Even though I'm still young, I've learned so much by going home at night and crying myself to sleep and just pouring my heart out to God in those moments. Through all of those times, I realized God was the best person to go to in those moments I needed comfort. Not to say my parents weren't there, but I strongly believe God allowed me to go through certain things so that I would run to Him more than anyone else. I never want to make my pain and hurt stop me from being myself and doing what I love, which is helping others. Be You On Purpose has helped me so much. I support and believe in it more than just because it's my mom's slogan. I see the impact it makes on the lives of others and it's amazing! I hope it also impacts your life as you read these stories.

-Brooklyn

*"Finding yourself is not
always easy when confronted
with your limitations,
but when strengths are discovered,
you become valuable
& confident."*

DeLana Rutherford

So my generation is a powerful one and I know this because most kids my age are already doing drugs and things of that sort. The devil tries to tempt us into doing these types of things and he puts it in our mind that if you smoke weed or have sex before you're married that its cool...but it's really not. We try to do these things because it seems like if we do it, we will fit in. Why would you want to fit in with that type of crowd? All they do is bring you down. To me standing out is way better because think about it...if you fit in no one will know who you are because you fit in with everyone. But if you stand out then lots of people will know you. Would you rather stand out or fit in now?

- Lyncoln

"The enemy can tempt you but he can't make your choices."

DeLana Rutherford

As I look back over my life, I realize that via pulpit, television and radio, I have ministered over 5,000 sermons. A sermon is more than just words from a pulpit – it's a life-coaching event that becomes the impetus for change in a person's life. When you consider this from the enemy's perspective…I'm a threat to the kingdom of darkness. Not surprisingly, Satan has attacked me repeatedly. Adversity and challenge will always be connected to great doors of opportunity. It goes with the territory!

Early in life, I was mandated with a very special calling. There wasn't an ah-ha moment: God did not audibly speak to me…I just knew! My father's desire was that I become a voice for God. When I was born, he prayed, "God…make him a preacher."

God granted my father's request, spoke to my heart as a child and developed a love in me for His word, but as many who are called tend to do, I ran from the call on my life. I didn't want to be a preacher! I wanted to be a rock star. I was into loud music, motorcycles, fast cars and electric guitars. I played in a rock and roll band for years, all the while feeling the conviction of my mandate. I wasn't convicted because playing rock music is sinful, it was because I was not following God's mandate for my life. In fact, I never got away from the call of God on my life; He would speak to me regardless of where I was or what I was doing.

Late one night, driving home from band practice, I heard the voice of God say, "You're on a dead-end street going nowhere." I resigned from my band that night.

Soon after, I met my wife, Yolanda. Our story is too long to tell here but she is a major part of the ministry I have today. Yolanda and I pastor Celebration of Life Church and God has given us many opportunities to minister to millions through Christian television and radio. In case you're wondering, my passion for music remains strong. Yolanda and I have released our latest project, "The JY Morgan Project – On the Move" which is a collage of R&B, gospel and jazz.

I enjoy ambitions and pleasures but my greatest sense of fulfillment comes when I am functioning in my God-given destiny.

- Joe

"When we go through things, it's not always about us. It's about who we are connected to that we are supposed to help."

DeLana Rutherford

I **asked the question**, *Why me God?* I was raised in a Christian home, served God all of my life and didn't understand why this was happening to me.

In 2002, while preparing for a conference, I became very ill and began to experience vertigo and nausea. The doctor diagnosed me with a severe sinus and inner ear infection and sent me home with an antibiotic to rest. The conference ended that Sunday morning and I still had vertigo and nausea, plus a tremendous headache.

Following the conference, my husband and I had plans to get away to relax for a few days. With trepidation, I began packing, although I remained aware of my sickness. Realizing I wasn't getting any better, I decided to call my doctor. He responded by increasing my antibiotics which I desperately hoped would make a difference.

I was admitted to the hospital and stayed for 27 days, enduring a battery of tests including eleven I.V.'s, five M.R.I.'s, and five spinal taps. Unfortunately, all the tests were inconclusive. My body was so worn and weak that I had no clue what was going on.

My husband never left my side. Late one night he heard me whisper, "My faith is healing me." Over and over again, I repeated it. I was not consciously aware of what I was saying, but my inner spirit knew exactly what to say.

After much testing, my doctor said, "Mrs. Morgan, I hate to give you this news, but we are diagnosing you with Multiple Sclerosis because of the lesions we found on your cerebellum."

I replied, "I do not receive this report. You have no idea the God I serve."

As I told you in the beginning of this story, the question I asked God while walking through this *Why God? Why me? After I have served you for years, why me?*

The answer was given to me one day during my desperation. I cried out to God and asked, *Why??* It was then that I heard the audible voice of my faithful God as He said, **"Because I knew I could trust you."**

That was twelve years ago. They said I would be in a wheelchair now but I am not. I wear six inch heels and enjoy life to the fullest! Are you believing for a miracle? Believe it will soon come to pass!

-Yolanda

"Hungry people that want God more than anything sacrifice & do whatever needed to get to Him!"

DeLana Rutherford

Where does one start in identifying just one miracle that God performed in your life? My life has been filled with miracles.

One of my sons flipped a Corvette for 300 yards after leaving the roadway at 140 mph. Arriving on the scene, I was told by rescue officials that my son died in the crash and the body had been taken away. On the way to the hospital I was near convulsions in agony over the news. God spoke to me clearly and said, "You give up too easily, Praise Me!" I began to praise Him in a very loud manner. The driver said he knew he had lost a grandson and I had lost a son, and now I would lose faith in God. Upon arriving at the hospital, a bloody ER doctor kicked a door open at the moment I walked in, saying "Who the #%@ is Rutherford?" I said, "I am!" He replied, "Get back here. Your son won't let me touch him until you pray with him!" Today my son has a scar in the back of his head as reminder of God's mercy.

In another instance, my wife and I were traveling an interstate. The Holy Spirit quickened me to stop and pray for one of our sons. Sue and I pulled off the side of the road and prayed for the dispatch of guardian angels and for Godly intervention. Later we were told that at that moment, my son and his wife were in distress in our private plane in a snow storm and icing up in Illinois. My son was able to get the plane on the ground without any incident except frayed nerves.

In another, a surgeon sat me down in a private room and told me that he didn't think he could save my wife from cancer. It was devastating. I made a decision to trust God, to refuse to believe the doctors report and not allow any negative remarks. After surgery, the surgeon said he couldn't believe that the cancer had not infiltrated her body. This year we celebrate our 51st Anniversary.

I was there when a Prophet called out my youngest son and said, "You are Myles, you are a Champion! You will minister to the multitudes!" Today, he does!

I could go on and on. Great is His Faithfulness!

-Lee

"Celebrate those who celebrate you."

DeLana Rutherford

What's important to you is important to God,

because we are His children.

It's been almost a year ago that Lee and I celebrated our 50th Wedding Anniversary with a trip to Hershey, PA and New York. I always wanted to visit Hershey, PA, stay in the Hershey Hotel and enjoy the city where the streetlights look like Hershey Kisses, with a Hershey Theme park and a Hershey Factory. My sister and her husband accompanied us. We also wanted to see "Moses" at the Sight and Sound Theatre in Lancaster, PA. It is a magnificent way to bring the Bible to life. On our last night, we ate dinner at an Italian Restaurant. Lee noticed a couple of guys looking at our jewelry which made him uncomfortable, so we left. Upon leaving the parking lot, he noticed that we were being followed, so we made some turns and lost them. When we got back to the hotel, I put my jewelry in a bag and didn't think about it anymore. We had a great time there and then headed for New York to meet a couple of friends. When we got to the hotel, I unpacked everything since we would be there at least a week. I opened my bag and took everything out of it. There was no ring. We searched everywhere to try and find the ring with no results. I was overwhelmed, not because of the money it cost, but the sentimental value connected to the ring. Ten years before, my husband took me to New York for my 60th Birthday. On New Year's Eve he presented that ring to me. We began to pray, our friends prayed, and our family prayed. I had peace that if we just believed, we would get an answer. We came home after our trip, called our insurance company and they began replacement proceedings. Early one morning a couple of weeks later, I walked into my closet. There on my Hassock, positioned face up was my ring, as if to say "Look what the Lord hath done!" My closet had been cleaned for two weeks, my clothes were hung up, suitcases put away, yet there it was. Lee and I were in AWE and very thankful. Listen, God knows every tiny detail about you, and if you ask and believe, He will answer and do great exploits for you.

-Sue

"Forgiving those who hurt you will free you more than them."

DeLana Rutherford

Living life beneath negative labels paralyzes purpose and incarcerates destiny. I'm the daughter of a Bishop, former administrator of a well-known ministry, and an ordained elder. However, none of these labels affected me positively because "DIVORCE" had its grip on every part of me. It was the first breath I breathed every morning and the last suffocating breath I gasped for at night.

I graduated college, was teaching school, serving faithfully in my church and thriving in life. I met and fell in love with what I thought to be the man of my dreams. We married, had two beautiful babies and then that dream turned into a disaster. My knight in shining armor turned into a dark, deceitful, distant person I didn't know anymore and definitely didn't like. Soon revelations of infidelities, confrontations, and abusive behaviors swallowed my dream into a twisted nightmare. Even more devastating, I couldn't tell anyone and risk people knowing that my life of perfection was now a huge insurrection. The fight for my life and the future of my family had just begun and I hadn't had time to get my gloves on good. I fought him, them, me, and failure and finally sitting in a small apartment with my two babies I got what I NEVER wanted...a final decree of DIVORCE.

Tonya Hall now meant DIVORCED. I remember entering my personal class of anger management trying to manage every emotion for my babies and always crying "Why?" to a dark silence that didn't answer. Or did it? The silence had an answer but I couldn't hear it through my anger, low esteem, abandonment, and zero confidence for me. I became excellent at empowering others and neglecting me. I rejected myself before others could. I gave my heart to helping others in any and every way. I resolved that I would die doing that not realizing God wanted me to live. Thank God for divine connections. Through a God-ordained pathway, I met and connected with the Rutherfords. Soon after, I ministered at their church and then a few months later their Gatekeepers Women's Conference, the birthplace of Be You On Purpose. Though I was a speaker on the flyer God's Grace found me in that atmosphere. Even now, I keep hearing the Holy Spirit chanting the words BE YOU ON PURPOSE....not divorce, not broken, not failure, not defeated, but the ME authentically God-designed not my design but God's design. I received the GRACE to live my life out loud, flaws and all. I no longer survive, I thrive. I realize life happens even for believers. I now live under a new label, "ME" and I realize more than ever God has purpose for ME.

- Tonya H.

"There's a difference between a strong woman and a Jezebel. Strong women know who they are and take control of their lives. Jezebel tries to control those who won't take control."

DeLana Rutherford

Insecure, bitter, depressed, angry and scared.

I was every last one of those things and singing. I was an adult trapped in the mind of a little 7 year old girl who had been traumatized by molestation, rape and neglect and I didn't know how to articulate my pain to anyone. All I knew how to do was bark and bite and my bite was vicious.

I would carry that pain for years until one day I heard the Lord say, "I've called you out of darkness into the marvelous light." It was in that moment, I knew I had to answer to the call or self-destruct.

I started answering that call every day at 5 am. I was determined to be free but that freedom came at a price…the price of comfort. There were days I would do more dozing off than praying, nodding than reading but I continued to push myself day after day, to soak in God's presence. It was a sacrifice with infinite benefits.

My thoughts soon became clearer. The suicidal contemplations began to vanish. My sadness was transforming into joy and there was a renewed peace starting to replace my ailing mentality.

At 39, I now sit in a chair about facing the world without hesitation, embarrassment or regret. I recite this line often, "Hi, my name is Lisa McClendon-Brailsford and I am an OVERCOMER, being me every moment, ON PURPOSE."

Lisa

"Anything unique and precious has to be crushed and pressed. Just like a diamond. You will shine again!"

DeLana Rutherford

I've seen a lot in 34 years. At the age of 5, I got molested by my youngest brother. At 9, I got raped by my paternal grandfather. Then at 18, I met my ex-husband who introduced me to heroin. I became an IV user, mixing cocaine and heroin to make what they call speed balls. At 21, we got arrested and he was sent to prison. I was put in a program where they help you kick the habit and started to live a normal life, or so I thought.

I started working at a restaurant where I met some "so called friends" and I got raped again. I had my first child in 2003 and my husband got released from prison. I started using heroin again and smoking crack to stay awake, popping pills, and shooting up meth. We got arrested again and I did 180 days. While on probation, I promised myself that would be the last time I used drugs.

In 2007, I met my two youngest children's father and got pregnant. I got into an argument and the cops were called, violating my probation, so I was 6 months pregnant and locked up. The state put me in a program where I could take my children with me but I was like a wild animal in a cage. A month later, I got arrested for beating another girl in the program. Three months later I came out with my son.

In 2009, my mother took me to court for custody of my children and was granted the right to adopt them. I started smoking marijuana to cope and during this time I met my current husband. On May 12, 2012, Mother's Day, I tried to commit suicide. I hit rock bottom and ended up in a white room at the hospital.

I would hear voices telling me I was no good, a bad mother, bad wife and I was going to die or be destroyed sooner or later. But, I would hear another voice telling me "You are my daughter, if you seek me I will do what I promised. I am the light and you need to follow me." I told my husband I couldn't do this anymore. In 2013, we came for vacation to see my sister and decided to move to GA and attend 3WC. I don't have my kids with me and can't see them, but I know it's because God is not done with me. I know one thing, I am free.

- Reina

"You can't be an approval addict and be free from what others think. You will never make them all happy."

DeLana Rutherford

I remember sitting 4 rows from the back of the church that Sunday as Pastor DeLana began to prophesy over another lady at the church. I was praying in agreement for her breakthrough, but she said something that stopped me in my tracks. She told the lady "...be YOU on purpose." I don't know what else she said that morning or even what was preached because those words were swirling around in my head. I couldn't stop crying, and I had to admit that I didn't know who I was. I knew how to be a daughter, a wife, a minister, a counselor, and a mother but I had no idea how to be ME. That Sunday put me on a journey of self-discovery.

You see, I wasn't an alcoholic or drug addict but I was bound by the opinions of people. Because I had no idea who I was, I became who others needed me to be or said I was. I was empty and always seeking approval and validation. This need made me vulnerable for people to use and abuse me which made me withdraw and have suicidal thoughts. It was like being molested as a child and the feelings of rejection all over again...a cycle of guilt and shame that wouldn't stop. Everyone saw my smile but they never looked deep enough to see my tears.

Through this "be YOU" movement, I found me and my voice. I found that the places I was trying to fill with people could only be filled with God. I learned to truly forgive others in my past, so that I could move forward in life. Where I was always a loner trying to protect myself, I have learned to open up to others. God has surrounded me with some amazing ladies that love me for me, not my gifts. Most of all, I have self-confidence. I know that I am fearfully and wonderfully made just the way I am and not ashamed of my past. I am not what I have been through. I am whole and FREE.

- Cassandra

"When you can share your story and the anger and pain is replaced with joy and peace, know you have been healed to help others."

DeLana Rutherford

My first memory as a child was looking in the mirror at the age of 3 and seeing a little monster looking back at me. My face was destroyed by a beating from my father. As I grew up, the abuse got worse by both parents from physical, emotional, verbal, mental, and a father who sexually molested me from the age of 6 until I was 12! During this time he became a pastor and I started maturing rather quickly. The thoughts that came to me were more like adult thoughts not that of a child. I would see my father in the pulpit and know that later he would be in my bedroom touching me and doing things I hated him for. I hated my father for taking away my innocence and hated my mother for not stopping the abuse and for participating in it.

I got hit with hammers, can openers, belts or a rubber hose while in the bathtub. I got bit, stepped on, slammed against concrete, and thrown through a window. So at 14, I started running away. I was too scared to go to the police because I thought no one would believe me. Every time I ran away they found me and I would get beat, but I got better at it. The last time it took them two weeks to find me. They came with the police and took me to a hearing. Everything they accused me of was a lie with the exception of running away. That's when they signed me over to the government and I was placed in a detention home. The anger and hatred grew even more! Now also against God! I ran away at 16 and found out my family had sold the house and moved to Puerto Rico.

I ended up in Puerto Rico and immediately got involved with a boy and got married at 17. I had 2 children but got divorced at 21. I was a single mom struggling with 2 babies and by the age of 35, I was homeless and needed quick money. A madam approached me, and I started prostituting. The money became addicting and my heart colder! I hated men. One day a client named Mario came to see me and we connected quickly. He was sent to finish the job by the devil. He was into witchcraft and was trying to lure me into that religion. In spite of my past, the seed that was planted in me would not let me bow down to the devil. Instead, I ministered to Mario and told him about my God! Me, a PROSTITUTE, ministering to a Santero! God has definitely used that double edge sword for both Mario and I. We have been in relationship with Christ since 2006 and free enough to tell you my story!

- Rebecca

"Learn to look in the mirror and embrace the YOU God made you to be."

DeLana Rutherford

I **went** *to* **the** **club** every night and church every Sunday...committing spiritual suicide. I have been in church most of my life and while my parents were not saved, I had a "praying Grandmother". One who made sure my sister and I were in church whether we liked it or not. This meant, I learned how to talk the talk, mimic the look and even fake the walk, but God knew my heart. It was far from trying to please him. I validated myself by being a "people pleaser". If it made others feel good, I did it. Which left me sexually abused, labeled as "fast", not knowing why I was that way and very broken hearted. I began to live a defensive life, where everyone and everything offended me and I felt like I always had to fight. I felt alone, lost and in an unidentified state. I didn't know who I was unless there was someone telling me who I was.

My lack of trust for anyone escalated as I grew older until there was no one that I would confide in. I drenched myself in the party life because it helped me to mask my emotions and form a permanent smile on my face. Although there were issues in my life that were overwhelming, no one would ever know because I had mastered the art of misrepresentation. I was not who people thought I was. I didn't even know who I was. I considered myself a chameleon because I was able to adapt to every situation that I was ever placed in. I presented a false sense of confidence but being you on purpose made me realize that there is no one, nowhere that could ever replace Maria. I am one of a kind and whether people like me or not, I have to remain consistent and be me. My experiences in life may have been tough at times, but they have shaped and molded me into exactly who I am supposed to be...ME!

- Maria

"When you embrace God,
you will eventually
embrace YOU."

DeLana Rutherford

There was an emptiness so deep inside, that kept getting filled with hatred and lies. It started with my parents' divorce, like any teen, I grew numb, of course. On the outside, I was fine, when I smiled, the whole room would shine. Yet, I felt so alone... I officially had no place to call home. Because the home that I knew, got torn into two.

We were always the closest, because I was daddy's little princess. Yet when there was the split, he moved states away & began to travel, and I began to unravel. My world began to twist and turn, the inner most parts of me started to burn, with anger and rage, yet I still felt stuck in this cage. With no escape and no way out, all I could do was scream and shout. But only on the inside, for it was implied, I had to be strong for my mother and sister, because of the pain, caused by that mister.

I continued to hide under fake smiles and laughs. Nobody knew me. They couldn't even see, that on the inside I was constantly dying, secretly crying out every night, "HELP ME!" I'd cry myself to sleep, then start a new day, without a peep. I was always that girl that was always forgotten. I would hear him say, "Oh, but I love you!" In my head I would think, "Really? Do you?" Cause you would have to prove it to me, in order for me to see past all the pain you've caused me.

I finally moved to college, thinking it would be my bandage, my get away, my escape from all the hurt from home, and from feeling so alone. Yet it started out worse, almost like an unknown curse. I still had to hide the real me, the side that I didn't want anyone to see. But here I was truly alone, I felt so lost, I didn't even know what paths to cross.

Then out of nowhere, God came and rescued me. No longer did I have to flee or hide the real me. I was truly free. Free from all the pain and anger. Free from all the hurt that always lingered. Free from trying to constantly fill that emptiness. All God needed was for me to confess, that I loved Him, and all I had to do was let Him love me...which wasn't easy, but somehow, HE turned out to be the best thing for me.

- Chandler

"When there is order
and obedience in your life,
there is peace."

DeLana Rutherford

I grew up around church. I knew who God was and I knew He was real, but couldn't see Him working in my life. My parents split when I was 9 or 10. My father was in and out of my life. It left me broken, hurt, and searching to find myself in all the wrong places. I searched to find love through sex and girls. I searched to find status and popularity through partying, drinking and smoking weed. I tried to find peace through a ball and a gym floor. I thought I had it all, but it wasn't until I had nothing that I found everything. Diagnosed with lung cancer at 17, my life was in pieces. I told myself there has to be more than what I've been doing. I'm so empty and broken! It was in that moment of brokenness that I began to be restored. I asked God to come into my life and gave Him everything I had.

I was blessed with a full scholarship to play basketball at Ohio University. I was ranked #56 at my position on ESPN and one of the top players in the state of Georgia. I thought I had made it! My dream of playing college basketball had finally come true. Little did I know God had a different path for me. I was at school for about 3 weeks and in those 3 weeks I didn't feel like I was living my dream. I spent day and night with God seeking His face and asking Him to help me find my purpose. It was then that I heard His voice calling me back home for ministry. I told my family, friends, and coaches what I was doing. I was pursuing the call of God, they would support and understand right? I got more push back and drama than I ever had in my life, but it was funny. The more drama and negativity I received the more peace I had about what I was doing. The more I heard "you don't know what you're doing!" The more I felt God saying "you're doing the right thing". It would have been easy to give in and keep my scholarship and pursue basketball, but I knew God and I knew what He said. I knew where I had my peace and I knew where I put my trust. I couldn't live my life according to other people, I had to live it according to where I had peace and by what God spoke and still speaks to me. It wasn't until I learned that principle that I was able to walk in freedom. Not bound by people's words, thoughts or actions. I walk with God every day and in Him I have found peace and freedom.

- Kendall

"Don't wait on others to ask for forgiveness. Forgive them first and be free!"

DeLana Rutherford

It all began when I was younger; the hurt, the pain, and the confusion.

About 10 years ago, my brother pursued me. I was young, so at the time I didn't really know how to deal with the situation, but I didn't have to for long. My mom wanted him to stay away from me but my dad felt like that was his son and he shouldn't be treated any differently. This was the start of every pain I've gone through. It was like I was the one child out of the family everyone wanted to take advantage of. I'm sure I wasn't the only one, but it felt like I was. I say this because, not to long after this, I was pursued by my cousin, who is a female. She asked a lot of me one night and we were so close and young I didn't really think much of it. Until I got older and I started becoming confused. This lasted from the 4th-7th grade.

I started to get more of an understanding of why I was confused, but from my peers. I noticed the spirit of confusion and loss of identity was taking over me. I figured if the spirit of homosexuality or confusion is going to be a part of who I am then I don't want to live. I stopped going to church for 5 months, my parents weren't okay, and I just felt like life wasn't worth it. So, I took the steps and attempted suicide. I was praying the whole time and asking God for a sign and to help me.

My best friend called and I dropped the bleach and surrendered. I will always remember that day because I realized I had a purpose in this world. I asked God to help me to forgive. It took a year, but God is always on time. I finally found my church home, where I found the Be You On Purpose woman's conference. At the conference, over the past 2 years I have gone, I have released both of my brothers and my cousin who pursued me. I have also forgiven my dad for leaving. I am honestly not the same person I was years ago. I found out who I am. Not in the world, but in Christ, and I'm not afraid to be me on purpose.

- Kiki

"Never let unhappy people decide what you are supposed to do."

DeLana Rutherford

At 15 years old, I watched my momma take her last breath after losing her battle with lung cancer. Ironically, she never once smoked. In the months following, I went from being happy and well-adjusted to being ridiculed with insecurity and fear. I would hear the whispers of adults saying that I would be a statistic of teenage pregnancy because my momma was no longer there. They never even knew I heard. My father, although physically present, had turned to drugs a couple of years before as a way of coping with losing his high school sweetheart, his wife and the mother of his 3 children. It would be years before I forgave him for what I believed was emotional abandonment. I was left with my sister, who was only 8 years older than me. Even to this day, she is still angry that she had to put her life on hold for me. I became obsessed with attempting to be "good". Anything that would cause my sister to be disappointed in me, I would not do. I didn't want her to leave me, too.

Tia was lost in every relationship. No matter the type. To most, I was confident and bold. However, inside I was a little girl desperately clinging to life and most days wanting it all to end. I was the little girl no one wanted. The little girl that no one stuck around for. My momma left. My daddy left. I wasn't enough for my momma to fight just a little harder. My daddy's addiction was stronger than his love for me. Simply put, I was not good enough. That's is what the enemy told me and I believed him. But my Heavenly Father would not relent. He stripped everyone and everything that I thought I needed. I was alone. At least, I thought I was. It was in those darkest hours that He showed me who I was in His eyes. He told me that He would be my mother and father. He has shown me that I could never be "good" enough. Yet, he would never leave or forsake me. Bit by bit, He restored me. He healed my wounds. Pretending to be confident is no longer needed. I now know who I am and WHOSE I AM. And because of Him, every day I am able to be Tia...on purpose!

- Tia

"be YOU...
no one else can
fit your shoe."

DeLana Rutherford

Fearfully and wonderfully made?

Growing up in a home with religious Caribbean parents wasn't easy. My parents migrated to the US and never adapted the American culture so things were different for me. I never received affection from my parents, I wasn't taught to embrace myself and I was always compared to family members when it came to my looks. My mother was very prejudice; being from a French mulatto and Dominican background she grew up believing she was superior in her country. So, not surprisingly we never lived in heavy populated African American communities so I wasn't introduced to the culture until my time in high school.

My nappy hair, big eyes and awkward shape always made me wonder where I came from. I was afraid of who I was so I imitated what I saw. I heard voices echo in my head "Be like them or you will be no one at all". What a nightmare! So many girls, so many shapes and sizes and all beautiful! What was wrong with me? Being a woman of color I believed you had to look a certain way so I began to eat everything in sight. I even went as far as asking my religious mother about putting me on birth control to gain weight to achieve this "African American look". I began to change my choice of music and extracurricular activities. I began to focus more on my looks and less on my purpose. I eventually became well known in my school but my new look didn't match the wholesome girl I was. Truth is I wasn't into losing my virginity, drugs or partying but I dressed for the role. I left high school feeling more confused about my identity.

I avoided women as much as possible after that and grew further away from friends and family, including my mother and sisters. In 2012, I made a last minute decision after talking with a friend, to attend a BYOPC. As I stood in the foyer surrounded by women, I suffered a major anxiety attack. I called my husband who began to pray with me and I mustered up the strength to walk through the doors. The panel that day spoke about identity and it was that day I understood who I was and the purpose I carried. Yes! I am fearfully and wonderfully made!

- Mary B.

"Never allow your emotions to dictate your future."

DeLana Rutherford

At a young age I always knew that God had placed purpose in me but what I didn't realize was that to reach my purpose I would go through pain. When I was two, my dad was addicted to drugs. I remember him coming home for a night and then when he would get ready to leave I would just hold him for as long as he'd let me, begging him not to leave because if he did there was always a chance I wouldn't see him for months. As I got older things got worse between my parents and they just couldn't seem to make it work so they got a divorce. I was so broken and angry with God because I didn't understand why he would allow me to go through so much pain. I desired to be close to my dad so much. I always wanted that daddy-daughter relationship but we always struggled to have that because his decisions always seemed to cause me pain. But when my dad got off drugs and I was healed from the pain of my parents' divorce, I really did realize that you have to love people more than you hate what they did. Now when I look at what I've been through it was so worth it. I have the most amazing relationship with my dad and mom. Everything I went through had a purpose and there was a plan behind all of it. Through it all I've always had God to lean on and He shows me every day how He sees me. Through that, I always trust that when I'm being me, I'm fulfilling my purpose.

- Lizzie

> *"You have to go to the root of the issue in order to be healed or delivered from what keeps you bound."*

DeLana Rutherford

My heart is beating faster than ever. The pixels of my curiosity are manifesting in front of me. My eyes are exhilarated with infatuation and my ears are tuned into the counterfeit sounds of love. It is extremely late, but who cares, I *need* to see more. I am safe. I can't get anyone pregnant. No one has to know, it's a secret.

Addiction had set root. It wasn't drugs. Not alcohol. No sexual intercourse. It was safe. Yet, it took complete control of me. No longer could I sleep at night, because my addiction would get the best of me. I always needed a fix.

It started in 8th grade and continued for what seemed like a life time. All I knew how to focus on was *not* sinning, but I didn't know how to move forward. Every night, I would cry myself to sleep knowing that I was a fake. Everyone viewed me as being perfect, so there was no way I could talk to anyone about my issue. I could not mess up my reputation, people were counting on me.

My life would never be the same. My thoughts and visions for my life would be corrupted with guilt and shame. Life as I knew it was a big fake. I would proclaim victory in the name of Jesus, followed by falling back into the same mess. What was I doing wrong? I prayed, I fasted, I went to church faithfully, I praised and I worshipped, and read my Bible. Yet, I could not shake this horrible and pleasurable sin.

One moment I would think that I was delivered and a few weeks later I was haunted with the same issue. Confronted by a trusted individual, I was able to release the fear and pain that was set inside of me. I became an overcomer and was empowered and reminded of who God called me to be. I learned how to trust again and believe not only in God, but in His people.

I am now living in my called purpose and divine assignment, because I am no longer focused on my sin, but instead focused on moving forward and being effective in God's Kingdom. I am by no means perfect, however I do not dwell on my weaknesses, for in my weakness He strength is made perfect. Now I am set free.

- Anonymous

"Dig deep to find the lost you.
It will be worth the pain
once you begin to heal."

DeLana Rutherford

I grew up fourth generation Pentecost. As a preteen, we traveled the country as Evangelists and our lives were centered on God and church. As a teenager, I suffered horrible depression for over two years. Because I was shy and insecure, I went on never speaking of it. I got married and within two years, I was separated and divorced. Slowly chipping away, a little more darkness enclosed around me. I knew all about God and who He was, but I didn't know who I was "in Him". I prayed and just kept going because that's what you do. Later, I remarried a "new" man and he would prove to be an amazing strength and love to me.

Then another piece of my armor chipped, and it shattered my heart. My parents separated and over the next several years I watched, I prayed, and I broke. Many nights I laid crumpled on the floor as the enemy also broke my father. We started finding reasons to stay away from church. I still had a heart for the Lord, but due to this and other situations, I was shutting down...more chipping and more darkness closing in around me. Finally they divorced. There was no saved ending or powerful answered prayer. I couldn't fix it. I was overwhelmed by the damage done to those around me and to my own soul.

By this point, I was just functioning. For six years the enemy came in to kill, steal and destroy. In 2013 my beloved Grandmother went into the hospital. I watched for almost two months as the one who had held me together so many times weakened. She passed away, but I promised her and myself I would get back to God. The enemy wasn't finished... Somewhere I found the strength to cry out to God.

I started going to Worship with Wonders Church, but not completely releasing my life to God. New Year's Eve 2013, we decided to live stream the service. I was sitting there on the couch defeated, broken, grieving, and lost in a fog. Anxiety surrounded me. Pastor Myles began to pray for the garments of 2013. He prayed for the past and what I had accepted into my life to be removed, then to put on new garments of 2014. The weight lifted off me immediately. I sat there crying as I received those words into my life. A few weeks later Pastors Joseph and Yolanda Morgan came and spoke into my husband and me. It was that moment where God steps in and you know it couldn't be anyone but Him. Our lives were changed and I am no longer the person who was sitting on the couch in 2013. Now I know who I am in God and I am learning to ...be ME on purpose.

- Trina

"Quit blaming your haters
& learn to change
YOUR mindset!"

DeLana Rutherford

A few years back I went through a separation and eventually got divorced. This was the hardest thing I'd ever done. I felt so alone, for a while, that I just had to get to a place and totally surrender to God for help. I had family and kids that I adored with all my heart, and I had to endure my pain as well as theirs. Now on my own, times were hard after being together for 30 years. I was feeling distraught with no direction. During that struggle, my path led me back to the Lord. I began to dig deeper into His Word for guidance. I was rebuilding a relationship that I knew I had, but needed now more than ever.

During my time of searching for new direction, I started writing, singing, recording, and kept trusting in God. I also wondered if there would be a soulmate for me. I was prophesied to and not long after that, I found the love of my life. He loves God with all his heart as I do.

So, for anyone out there that ever thinks that it will not work out, let me tell you when you totally put God first it will. I know everyone's situations are different, but GOD is not prejudice to your situation. He loves you and wants you to know Him. I continually live my life serving my God. He is my best friend, my healer, my peace maker, my provider, my everything. Be YOU on purpose!

-Brauninger

"*Understand your passions and they will guide you to your purpose.*"

DeLana Rutherford

What I was running from, I ended up running into!

I had "everything" a man could imagine. The feeling of being on top of the world, performing on stages, and promoting some of the hottest night clubs. For years, I struggled with filling an empty void in my life with girls and drugs. This included cocaine, methamphetamines and pills. I did anything possible to fit in with the dealers, from selling drugs, robbing folks, and collecting debts owed (in any manner possible). I joined a gang and moved my way up in the ranks quickly. I was well known to the local police department, Drug Task Force and peers on the streets. I've seen and done things that people on death row could associate with.

Then I hit rock bottom. Everything I had worked for in my life was gone. I was left all alone... money gone, so called "friends" abandoned me, and I had a little girl whose daddy was no longer around. At one point, I was homeless. I was lost, still trying to fill that empty void. Six years addicted to meth, I finally realized what I was really running from...my calling.

I was scared of how powerful my mind actually was, how I had the ability to inspire so many people around me, so I hid from myself.

People have always told me I was a leader not a follower. I started cleaning up my act. I moved to Florida in 2008, leaving the drugs and pills behind. However, there was one thing I couldn't let go of. I was still bound by alcoholism. I left a club, with a so called "friend" one evening, next thing I remember was waking up in the hospital with stitches down the front of my head. From my understanding, my "friend" was the cause of the accident; I had two major seizures, one stopping my heart.

July 2, 2011, I was fed up with that lifestyle and needed change. I jumped in my truck, still drunk from the night prior, and headed to Georgia. My sister invited me to her church, Worship with Wonders, and I gave my life to Christ. I haven't been the same person.

Now I serve as head of security and pastoral assistant. Running right into my calling as a preacher!

- George

"Find your lane, and get in it,
and drive - at your pace."

DeLana Rutherford

I was a hurt little girl trying to find love. I had a mother that worked all of the time and had no father figure at home. Mom was single. I would allow the boys to take advantage of me because I thought that would make them love me. I was like that as an adult too. I then found myself in a relationship with my "PRINCE CHARMING". He was beautiful and published a magazine. He was everything I thought I could ever want in a man right? Wrong! He was addicted to porn and sex with other women. My heart was broken over and over. I felt worthless, ugly and like nobody would want me because I didn't look like the girls he masturbated to or talked to online every night. So I had identified with what the enemy was trying to make me believe about myself. I felt like I would never be able to make any man want me. I drank every night and got on all of the dating sites. I posted pictures of myself all over my social media walls in order to get validation from men. I finally realized that I couldn't be happy trying to fix my heart on my own. I surrendered everything to Christ. He loved me back to life. I realized that I am worthy. I am beautiful! I am everything that makes Jesus love me... I am His princess! He makes me feel like a princess! I didn't need to look for prince charming anymore because I found Him. He was there all the time and His name is Jesus. I am actually living happily ever after.

-Mary J.

"Keep loving the unlovable...
It's freeing YOU more
than you know..."

DeLana Rutherford

I was in love with Lance and he was in love with me. I never found anyone that loved me the way he did. He loved everything about me, but it took me a long time to love him back because I was so hurt after the loss of my 13 year old son. Everything was good, except he did not believe in Jesus Christ. He had studied with Muslims, 30 years ago, and thought Jesus was just a prophet. He knew the Bible inside and out, but I knew I could not marry anyone that didn't believe in Jesus. God had brought me through so much when I lost my two sons, but I stayed in the relationship until finally I broke it off.

We got back together after he told me that he knew Jesus Christ was his Lord and Savior. He said he could see what He was doing in my life. I truly believed he believed it, but he just wanted to marry me. One day his nephew asked, "Uncle Lance is Jesus Christ your Lord and Savior?" and he said, "No he's not my Lord and Savior." Once I heard that I knew I could never marry him. We continued to be friends until I realized that I was wasting a lot of time. I also did not want to get in trouble with the Lord. He assured me he was trying but there was always excuses why he wasn't going to church and always worked on Sundays.

I realized I was angry because he wasn't the person I thought he was. He said he was trying and on January 12, 2015 the police knocked at my door and asked me did I know a Lance? I told them yes, but he didn't live here. They asked me to contact Grady Hospital. I reached out to his sister and she told me when she got there he was gone. The cause of death was a heart attack. All I thought about was did he make it into heaven.

At the funeral, I met his cousin, a Pentecostal minister, from New York. As we talked about his beliefs, her words were, "I keep hearing God say I took him when I had him!" After talking to her and another cousin who had been reading him the Bible, I am so glad to know that God can save someone at the time of their belief!

-Cynthia

*"When you find the real you,
you won't need others' approval.
You find an inner peace and
confidence that will change your life!"*

DeLana Rutherford

"Be YOU on purpose..." I heard this statement

all the time, but I couldn't seem to figure out which "ME" I should be. I never had a clear understanding of who I was or whose I was, so I allowed other people to define me based on what was convenient for them. Molested at the age of twelve, I looked at the world through the eyes of lost innocence. As the loneliness and shame from that experience consumed me, I started searching for anything that could offer some sort of relief, comfort and explanation. That search led me to a counselor who told me it was clear that I was a lesbian and that my life would be much easier if I accepted that fact and moved on. I didn't even know what that meant, but since I didn't know ME, I accepted what I was being told and embraced a lifestyle that was far too happy to embrace me.

As the inner turmoil ensued from what I had been taught was right and what felt right to me, the only real thing I knew was the hatred I had for myself. I turned to cutting to try and bleed out the emotional poison but it merely left me with physical scars to match the ones I had on the inside. But then I picked up my Bible and started reading the greatest love letter ever written. I began to see trails of unconditional love that I had been taught didn't exist for sinners like me. The more I read, the more God started speaking to me on a personal level and drowned out all the hatred I felt in the past. I'd always thought I had to fix myself before God could love me and since I couldn't get it right, I didn't believe I deserved His love. But as I kept hearing "be YOU on purpose..." I was determined to get to know exactly who it was God had created me to be. I embraced His love for me and that I was fearfully and wonderfully made in His image and began to shed all the images that other people had put on me. The moment I stopped trying to fit into the box that people placed me in was the moment I got to know the real me and was able to be ME on purpose!

- Nicole

*"God created YOU
just like you are. Learn to embrace
everything about YOU!"*

DeLana Rutherford

It all started when my father left. Seven years old was an early age to comprehend what was truly going on, but it began to take its toll as I got older. Since there was no male figure to fill the void my father had left, I ended up looking for acceptance and love in guys when I entered middle school. Insecurities then consumed me as I tried to become what I thought boys wanted. These unrealistic expectations took a turn for the worst when the idea of skipping a few meals to lose weight turned into what would be a 4 year battle with anorexia. This disease then took over my life, and I was no longer Talen, I was my eating disorder. Depression walked into my life, and not too long after that, I was introduced to self-harm. At first it was just when I was upset, but nobody told me it would become addicting. That first cut opened up a door to a whole different world. In this world I was in control. This addiction grew into a daily routine, no matter how I was feeling. The physical pain took away from the mental nightmare I was going through each day. Suicide slowly made its way into the darkest place of my mind, and with every cut was the thought of, "Just end it now".

As I rapidly spun out of control, my family realized how bad this situation really was. I was put into rehab at 14, where I was not allowed to go outside, slept on a bed in the hallway, and had no connection to the outside world other than three visits a week from my mom. I was given multiple medications until the psychiatrists found the right combination of three that would maintain the chemical imbalance in my brain that was causing my sickness. Once I got out of treatment, I still self-harmed as well as continued my eating disorder. It wasn't until I was saved 2 years ago that I realized I was of priceless value. God gave me the strength to come off each one of my medications, cold turkey. Side effects of doing this were a big risk, but I went through withdrawal with no relapses and stayed clean by the grace of God. Without God, I know for a fact my disease would've won. He turned my pain into my story. I now help girls who were just like me, and my testimony has not only helped them, but saved their lives. God gave me a reason to keep fighting, to keep breathing. He gave me a purpose.

-Talen

"Being free is living life to its fullest!"

DeLana Rutherford

My relationship with God was non-existent. I went to church because that's what I was supposed to do. During my time in Iraq as a soldier, I felt closer with God than I had ever felt in my life. One night a bomb hit close to my room. The time it hit I would have normally been in bed, but that day I had to stay at work late to finish a report. When we heard the first bomb hit we all were saying, "Wow that was close". Then the second one hit. We looked out the door and saw that the smoke was coming from the direction of our rooms. We put on our gear and ran over. I went to my room and saw the damage. Had I been in the room I would have been seriously injured or maybe killed.

I thought after that situation that I would never lose my closeness with God. I felt like God had planned the events of MY day to keep me out of my room that night. I really felt like I was in a real relationship with Him where I could just talk to Him anytime and He would hear me clearly.

Once I returned from Iraq I went to a church that my family was attending. I lost myself right away, going back to that feeling of not having a relationship with God, just going to church because that's what I was supposed to do. Doing things I knew were not pleasing to God, not praying, not reading the Bible, listening to music that was crazy, cursing and having sex was the biggest thing. Then I got pregnant and had my first son. I honestly can say I went like 2+ years without praying or talking to God. I found Worship with Wonders and started coming while still attending my other church. Pastor DeLana asked me several times if she could pray for me and I refused. After about 3 months, at a Wednesday night service, she asked me again and I said yes. When she laid hands on me I couldn't fight the Holy Spirit anymore. The guilt that I had for having a child, for not having a relationship with God went away INSTANTLY, and for the first time in 2 years I felt like I was free to worship again, free to pray again, free to be the Chalese from Iraq again.

- Chalese

"People who are driven by emotions
will never be consistent
in their purpose."

DeLana Rutherford

I am a single mother who has been faced with many obstacles over a 2 year span. One cold winter day I was driving down a hill and my car slipped on some ice. I was the 4th car in a 5 car pileup. I was diagnosed with a concussion which completely wiped my vocal chords away for 1 ½ weeks.

Several months later, I was still going back and forth to the doctors for migraines and dizziness. Shortly after that, I blacked out, fell and hit my head on something metal. Once again, I was diagnosed with a concussion. My speech went away instantly and came back in 1 ½ weeks.

A few months after that incident, I was driving on I -75 taking my daughter Maya Imani to her book signing and out of nowhere an 18 wheeler truck hit me. I remember thinking Lord no, please don't let this be the end with the kids in the car. I was scared for my life. When the ambulance got there, they said I was in shock and once again I had another concussion and my speech left me. I was hurt, my car was totaled and I was in total silence. I had to recover and thank my God that we were all alive. This was a very difficult time for me and it gave me time to rethink things.

Five months later, I had a stroke. I am too young to have a stroke. I am just 38 years old. Be you on purpose means I keep going, keep believing, and keep striving for who God says that I am. Being me on purpose means to keep walking in my destiny, keep fulfilling the call on my life, and it means to live life. I've got another chance to be who I want to be now, to stand up for something right and to not be timid.

- Jawana

"Never compare yourself to others
and feel you don't measure up.
Every single person has
their own process.
We are built to go through
our own."

DeLana Rutherford

Be you on purpose means...to laugh everyday... to do things that make you feel good...to give away things...to have fun with your friends...to love your church...to dance...to sing...

I was born with Congenital Band Syndrome 17 years ago. It is where my full arm and hand didn't grow out I have a partial left arm. Growing up I was picked on and bullied to the point I had to be homeschooled. On top of that, I had a daddy who was nowhere to be found. He has never been in my life. I, at one time, was suicidal but I couldn't let myself do it. I never did have those thoughts again because of the grace of God.

Be you on purpose has helped me. The teens have gotten together in a group and have talked about some things that was on our hearts. We have had lock-ins, and conferences which helped us to get things off of our chest. Be you on purpose is not just for teens it's for everybody.

- Maya

"You can sleep when you're dead. Dream & work now."

DeLana Rutherford

From the first time the words "be YOU...on purpose" were spoken to me, it fueled a desire that moved me to truly start being me on purpose! I was so inspired that I asked permission to print these words on a t-shirt. I wanted to express myself in this way even though I felt invisible. I have always loved wearing t-shirts with unique sayings. Wearing t-shirts was a way for me to express myself, while living in a world where I felt invisible or if anyone saw me/remembered me it was only because of the scars on my face. So, after hearing this cool Pastor constantly say "be YOU on purpose", it resonated with me. I said "I will be me on purpose" and it doesn't matter who sees the real me because my Heavenly Father is watching and He did not make a mistake. This journey to being me on purpose has been amazing! Those four words have changed my life. I understand I am relevant. I am beautiful. I am smart. I matter. Now I am not only being me on purpose, I am being me *with* purpose!

-Tiffany

"Don't hold a grudge so long that it becomes a lifestyle handed down to the next generation behind you. Free you & them!"

DeLana Rutherford

Having a very rough childhood, being raised by a hard-working single mom and a paralyzed grandmother, ended up leaving me to become a ward of the state when both died. This left me as an angry and radical youth. It was evident that I was a challenge, since most of my case workers quit and I was an unsettling nomad runaway from foster homes. Cop cars were my taxi ride back to where I belonged. I was full of hatred toward humans and truly hated myself. Being a raisin in the sun, didn't help matters especially in school.

When my mother was alive, the pressure was so great for her that she sought guidance from sorcery, especially for me and my future. The only crystal ball reading that stuck to my memory was at a certain age all that was seen was a bright light and nothing was seen past that. It troubled my mom that it could mean an early death.

Music and my pet boxer were my only relief, until I hooked up with the wrong crowd. Then drinking and pills were my comfort. Those who became my friends ending up overdosing. I mourned but was happy thinking they were in a better place than me. Trying suicide 3 times never worked for me, so I gave up.

God's intervention came when the family I am now grafted into, showed the enduring tough love that nursed me to health. Coming into a personal relationship with Jesus, led me on a journey that would take a book to write. Like peeling an onion, one layer at a time, the Lord has done a transformation on my life that has truly made me a new creature in Christ.

When Pastor DeLana began the Be You On Purpose Movement, there were still areas that needed to be addressed in my heart. I can truly say that this line and precept came timely and has made me more of a confident woman. I can see that all that I went through can be seen shamelessly and shared as a source of strength to others.

The fervent love I have now, outweighs the strength of hate I carried for years. I am beginning to show love and kindness and hospitality without measure. I realize that however I treat others, I am doing as unto God.

I am comfortable being me on purpose now.

- Chrissie

"Whoever has your ear,
has your destiny."

DeLana Rutherford

My parents took me to church every time the doors were open. Fast forward, I'm now 21, single, faithfully serving God, and waiting for Him to send me "the one". Then one Sunday in walks, "the one". His worship was genuine, his excitement contagious, and from that moment on we were inseparable.

But after 8 long years of empty words, broken promises, verbal and physical abuse, I realized that this couldn't be what God had promised me. Somehow I found the strength to end it, but I felt like a failure. After years of changing myself to become what I thought he wanted, I had lost my identity.

Shortly after, I lost my dad to cancer. He loved me like no one else ever had. For this daddy's girl, losing him left me feeling angry, and empty. I couldn't understand how a God who supposedly loved me could allow me to suffer such heartache. So I pushed God to the side and lived my life for me.

I looked for anything that could make me feel something. I was tired of feeling numb. I wanted to be loved, to belong to someone. Then I met someone who desired me, and once again I gave him my body, my heart, my soul. This relationship didn't last long and then there was another, and another. Eventually I realized the only time I felt something was when I was having sex. Thankfully after months of emptiness, hurt and anger, God opened the door for me to come to Worship with Wonders.

When I heard about the "Be You..." movement something began to stir in me. I would hear women talk about knowing who they are in Christ and all the things He had delivered them from, and my heart longed to feel the same. After getting in His presence, and asking God's forgiveness, especially for my anger towards Him, I started to feel free. After years of giving myself away, God used "Be You..." to show me that nothing in my life is a mistake. All of my desires, my talents, my likes/dislikes, were all chosen by Him and placed within me ON PURPOSE. He continues to reassure me that He has me where He wants me and that His plans are not to harm me, but to give me a future and a hope. I am now able to confidently love myself, knowing that my Father made me exactly the way He wants me, and He doesn't make mistakes.

-Rachael

*"When you are truly broken,
you will have more
grace for others!"*

DeLana Rutherford

I was blessed at birth. I had the most functional childhood possible. A God-fearing mother that made sure I was saved at 14 years old. A dad that taught me the facts of being a hard worker and doing the things a man should.

People generally say that the reason someone starts using drugs is because something happens to you, like a trauma. With me, that didn't happen. I was a young boy that was saved, walked out the door, and was attacked by the devil. At 15, I started drinking and at 16 I was on drugs. By 18, I was married with two children. Drugs haunted me off and on most of my life. By all rights, I should have died, but I now know God watched after me. He had a purpose for me way later in life.

During my marriage, I was physically and mentally abused for 21 years. I could not stand the thought of losing my children so I stayed. During this time, I continued to smoke pot. Even though I was so far from God, He still watched over me. After years of abuse, she admitted she had always been an adulteress wife. God had freed me from that abusive marriage.

Now alone, God sent me a GREAT new wife. You would think this would change me. No. My wife was a recovering addict and I was still smoking pot. I am so ashamed to say we both got on meth at 38 years old. Only coming to near death was I able to get off meth. The pot smoking continued until two years ago.

A few years prior to this my grandson was sexually abused. This consumed me with hate. God sent me a friend and she convinced me to write my story about my grandson. Then God started really dealing with me on many things like not going to church, cursing, anger and pot. It got so strong that I could not ignore it. Smoking a joint one night God spoke to me and I simply said, "God take this urge from me". I felt it leave my body. Jesus can heal you from drugs. Once an addict always an addict is not true. I am proof of this.

- Michael

"Never live in your past,
but don't be afraid to look back
and use it for God's Glory."

DeLana Rutherford

At 11 years old, I was run over by a drunk driver. My dad pulled over to fix a flat tire and I stood at the back of the car when suddenly I saw another car coming straight toward us. I screamed for my dad, which was the last thing I consciously remember until months later. I was drug under the car, face down on the concrete. Mom immediately got out to pray for me, but neither ambulance paramedics nor the ER Doctors gave me any hope of living.

My family would not accept negative reports and only allowed praise and worship music to play in my room at all times. After 3 months, I remember the nurses standing in amazement as I walked, since the day before I wasn't able to do anything but remain in a vegetative state. What the enemy intended for my death and failure is now my life and testimony.

Even more life changing was meeting the driver of the car that hit me. After 10 years, I wanted to meet her and see if I was able to forgive her. Little did I know, the process God was taking me through had little to do with me and ended up changing her life as well. I woke up one morning praying about meeting her. I wrote my prayer down and as I began to wait on God, my prayer became more for the driver than me. I wrote, Lord give her a new life, a reason to live. Take away her shame. Help her to forgive herself and so on.

When we arrived at the center, I immediately looked her in the eye and told her my name. She immediately began crying. I told her I forgave her. The very first words out of her mouth as she sobbed were "I was going to commit suicide on Sunday but now I have a new reason to live". She told me that she hadn't had alcohol or drugs since the day she hit me. She was president of her Alcohol Anonymous Club, but was still going to commit suicide that weekend until she knew forgiveness. Not only did she realize I forgave her and God forgave her, she realized she could forgive herself.

Two days later, on the Sunday she planned to commit suicide, she came to our church. My dad who was the Pastor introduced her as my new friend. Not only did the healing take place in me, in her, and my family but all those connected to us. God restored her life. One year later she sent me a picture and what used to look sad and lifeless looked full of life and purpose. We remain in touch and I cannot tell what a blessing it is to call her my friend and see the miraculous work God has done in both of us.

- Sherry

"Surround yourself with people who believe in you and can push you to your destiny."

DeLana Rutherford

I grew up with supportive parents who introduced me to sports at a young age. I continued to play sports all through high school, earning accolades for my athletics and academics. I only made a B on my report card one time my whole life. I finished third in my high school class while being offered multiple scholarships to play football in college. I was a model young man. The one that all the parents wanted their daughters to bring home.

Late in my high school career, I started doing a little drinking and smoked a little bit of weed. It was just recreational at that point. Out of fear, I chose not to play football at the collegiate level. Instead, I stayed home and enrolled in Kennesaw State University. This is when my drinking and drugging started to increase. Before I could blink, I had been arrested for DUI and lost a job because of my drug use. I was still able to keep myself together. No one knew of the struggles I was going through.

I later found success in the restaurant business. I worked my way up to a General Manager position with a high end restaurant. This would be where my drinking would catch up to me. Although all of my legal troubles came from the alcohol, I received a felony drug charge that turned out to be a blessing in disguise. This cost me my job and almost took my life. I didn't have much of a reason to live so thoughts of suicide and one minor attempt plagued my thoughts.

The blessings started when I got accepted into the Cobb County Drug Court Program. I sobered up enough to slow down and gather my thoughts. I always believed there was a God but had no interest in a relationship with Him. At my rock bottom, I asked God to take control over my life. I knew He couldn't screw it up worse than I had. The very night of me rededicating my life to Christ, He showed me He was real. A MAJOR struggle that I was dealing with through drug court was immediately wiped away.

Through this process God lead me to 3WC to do community service. Pastors Myles and DeLana were the first people to look at me during my transformation and tell me that I was destined to be successful. I know God used them to give me HOPE. From that point forward I found so much motivation to reach for the dreams that I had for my life. Since then, God has completely restored me and the things I lost in my life. I continue to serve HIM today and forever!

-Brandon

*"God will always equip you
for your purpose if you
are willing to make
the sacrifice."*

DeLana Rutherford

$\mathcal{M}$*y story is* one that you hear far too often these days – one of pain and the loss of someone you love. In my case, it was my wonderful husband of 33 years, Ed.

He and I were both blessed to have been raised in Pentecostal homes by Godly parents who were strong in their faith and raised us to be strong Christians. So, when he was diagnosed with cancer-lymphoma, we stood strong in our belief that God would heal him. I never doubted. Imagine how it felt when two months from the day of his diagnosis God took him home. Your mind cannot comprehend what has happened. Your heart physically hurts and everything in your world has changed...except God.

I attended my first "Be You" conference two years after I lost my husband. At the two year mark, you're realizing that it's not a nightmare. The one you love is not coming back. The second year without them is even harder than the first. It was refreshing to be in each service and to feel His presence washing over me. I left the conference feeling stronger spiritually than I had for several years.

The week before the 2014 conference, the Lord gave me a song entitled "In His Arms". The chorus says "In His arms I'm forgiven, In His arms I am free, In His arms I can BE WHO I AM." And that's what I'm learning more and more each day. I can be who He's called me to be. This is not where I thought I'd be in life, but God knew before I was even born that I would be here and His love and strength will help me be who He needs me to be.

Through the "Be You" conferences I have gained the strength to continue in the work of the Lord. I am in the process of publishing my first book called "Even If...Trusting in God even if the unthinkable happens." I believe it will encourage those who have lost someone they love. I don't know where He's leading me, but I know I can still trust Him!

Thank you Pastor DeLana for your love and support and for the "Be You" experience!

- Deborah

"When God delivers you,
you must walk it out daily
as you conquer every trigger that
would set you back."

DeLana Rutherford

According to the world's view, I grew up as a statistic. I was raised in a fatherless household. However, I had a wonderful mother that did the best she could to raise me and my older brother as a single parent. With the help of my late great-grandparents, who were pastors, I was brought up in church and given a little more stability. My mom worked multiple jobs to make sure that she provided financially for both my brother and I, but of course that meant that most of her time was spent at work and less on parenting. I harbored fear and anger for most of my life.

As a result of not having a father and sense of security, I began to do things to try and conquer my emotions. I found comfort in drugs and sexual experimentation. Unbeknownst to my mom and grandparents, and still in church, I turned marijuana and homosexuality. At the age of twelve, I was introduced to marijuana and found comfort in the feeling of being high and having my fear and anger go away, momentarily. I constantly felt the need to turn to the drug at any moment that I felt fear, stress, low self-esteem, loneliness or anger. I always knew that I was loved and supported by my family, but not having my father was very hurtful. Most times I put on the facade that it had no effect on me.

Also, at the age of twelve, I was molested by a longtime family friend until I was 15. Still being bound by fear, I never told my family. That was my introduction to homosexuality. I was scared, nervous, and confused. As the molestation happened repeatedly, dysfunction became normal. I was manipulated into thinking that this lifestyle would fill the void of not having a father around. But, thanks be unto God who always causes us to triumph in His name, I can say that I am no longer a victim to drugs or homosexuality. With God's strength I was able to forgive my father and find the validation that I needed. God delivers!

-Antony

"Broken people CAN heal others."

DeLana Rutherford

It happened too soon...

I became a mom at the age of 16. Out of curiosity, and engaging in sex for the first time, I became pregnant. This one moment of wanting to know changed my life forever. After I had my son, it didn't take me long to realize that I was not ready for this. I was not focused on caring for a child. I had the mind of a little girl, who just stopped playing with dolls a year ago.

I ran from my role as a mother. Of course, I loved my son. However because of my immaturity, I was not aware of how to show it effectively. I went to college and my mom cared for him while I was away. I visited him on the weekends, when I wasn't partying.

At 17, my definition of a mom was work and make sure he had food, clothing and shelter. My mom was providing shelter so, I worked to send money home to her while I was in college. I did this until he was 3 years old. At this time I began to develop my relationship with God. He revealed to me that not knowing who I am through Him was pushing me further away from my son. Not long after that, I overcame the fear of being a mother and moved him with me full time.

I was scared, afraid, and many times felt alone because I didn't know what I was doing. I began to watch other mothers and pattern my parenting styles after theirs. It wasn't long after that God said again, not knowing who you are through me is pushing you further away from your son. The second time I heard this the light bulb came on. I understood that He wanted to show me who I was in him so I could be the parent He has created me to be to my son.

I am not saying do not to seek advice from other parents, but I had to develop my relationship with God so I can discern when I am receiving the correct advice. As a result of now knowing who I am through the eyes of God, as a young parent raising a pre-teen no longer scares me, it reminds me that God has equipped me. Pastor DeLana put the icing on cake with the "be you on purpose" movement. I am being the best single mom to my children "on purpose"

-Ashley

"If you don't have a Godly heritage, start one now. It's never too late to change your legacy."

DeLana Rutherford

I was just like the average kid with no worries until my parents divorced when I was 6. I didn't understand it so it didn't have much of an effect...or so I thought. I started acting out and being rebellious. I wasn't angry or sad but I knew my parents were separated and I could get away with certain things...like smoking weed for the first time at age 9. This went on for some time but I never got into serious trouble, simply because my parents didn't really believe in disciplining me.

At 12, my dad murdered his wife at the time. I thought they were madly in love, but using cocaine and being diagnosed with depression, one day he just snapped I guess. That hit me hard because he was the only person I looked up to. Less than a month later, my favorite cousin was shot and killed at the age of 15. That was devastating and confused me quite a bit. My mother, trying to raise 3 fatherless kids alone and battling her own depression, eventually got addicted to crack when I was 14. At 15, I started selling drugs and robbing people. I've been to jail and on probation, been robbed at gunpoint and involved in numerous shootouts.

My brother and I were tight because I've taken charges for him. We were inseparable until one day he did a robbery without me. He beat a guy to death and was sentenced to 40 years in prison. There was a pattern, a generational curse I couldn't shake that made me rebel more and my heart grow colder. Everybody that I loved and looked up to ended up leaving some way or another, so I decided I would look up to nobody but myself. Trying to be a "leader", I built a power team and recruited my two little cousins to be part of my squad. All I was selling was marijuana and my mindset was, weed can't be that dangerous. But living a worldly lifestyle is always dangerous. It cost my little cousin's life 18 days before his 21st birthday over a couple $100 of marijuana. It should've been me making that sale but I was out of town and told him to go instead. It took 13 years of losing everyone I loved, but that day I finally realized that I needed to change.

I humbled myself and let GOD handle my situation. I was running from HIM trying to figure out life and ended up running to HIM for all the answers. GOD wanted to use me, that's why I was allowed to go through so much and still be here to tell it. Giving my life to GOD was the best decision I've ever made. I don't stress or lose sleep over anything because I know GOD is my strong tower. It's never too late to make a change. We are chosen by GOD to lead the world towards the light. I believe GOD will restore everything lost in those years I was blind.

-Laris

"Finding you is finding purpose."

DeLana Rutherford

I am a small town girl born and raised in Southern Illinois all my life. My parents divorced at the age of 12 and my mother left my brother and me with our dad. We would go months without hearing from her at times. Growing up, my paternal grandmother had so much influence in my life. I give so much credit to her as to why I am who I am today. At 20 years old, still trying to figure out what to do in life, I had my first child, Chassidy Leigh. Then at age 26, I had my second child, Skylar LaRae-both fathered by the same man. It was a very tumultuous and abusive relationship. He was a drug abuser and woman abuser.

After fearing for my life, I was able to leave the relationship. In the midst of that relationship though, I started going to church with his family and at the age of 25 knew there was something missing. I knew I needed Jesus and I found him. Being a babe in Christ, I struggled a few years in my relationship with God.

Later at the age of 31, I met a man and married. Not long after we met, my oldest daughter, Chassidy, age 12 was diagnosed with Acute Myelogenous Leukemia. The weight of the world was on my shoulders, trying to stay with a sick child and having another 6 year old child at home to find relatives and friends to care for during the course of her illness. After 10 short months of treatment, Chassidy passed away.

To deal with my grief, I invested myself into something positive and began nursing school. I graduated from nursing school in 2008. I continued on being a mom to Skylar and two step-daughters, a wife, and a full time nurse. After irreconcilable differences, my husband and I divorced in 2012. Later, in October that year my 15 year old daughter, Skylar, took her life one night at home. I have not been the same since.

Later, I moved to Georgia for a fresh start. After Skylar passed away, the enemy tried to convince me I had no purpose in life anymore. Due to the devastation I had experienced, I almost bought the lie. I was driving down the road one day mad at God, broke and cried and said, "GOD I NEED YOU!" I have had many stressors that are listed at the top of the charts in my life, but as I look back I know my Lord and Savior has carried me through it all. My God has shown me I do have a purpose here and now I am being me on purpose!

- Tonya B.

*"Stop running
with fruit killers."*

DeLana Rutherford

My name is Hayden and I am sixteen years old. My parents divorced when I was about four years old and I went to live with my mom from there. My life was pretty steady and normal just like any other child. I was like every other kid growing up saying "I will never do drugs" but that mindset abruptly changed.

I was about thirteen years old the first time I did a drug which was marijuana. I was with some friends who had done it a few times before and said it was harmless; so I did it...and did it and eventually it turned into an everyday thing.

Eventually I started throwing parties in the shed in my backyard. I started drinking alcohol and doing other drugs. A year later when I was about fourteen I threw a party in my shed like I did just about every weekend. There were about twenty people there that night and one of my friends had these over the counter pills that if you took too much of it would get you high. I took the pills and I was drinking alcohol with them, which all of us know those do not mix well together. I did it anyways, and around an hour later, I started feeling the high but it didn't feel right. Eventually I couldn't stand up without falling, when I tried to talk I would slur my words, and my vision was very blurry.

It kept getting worse and worse as time went on. The main thing I remember that I will never forget was me lying on my bed with everyone around me and I honestly believe I died for a few seconds. My eyes closed while I was lying down and all I remember is this white light and this big golden gate with a guy in front of it saying "Hayden, I will give you one more chance". That man was God and those were the gates of heaven; I know that and I know that God is real, I've seen him and experienced him. I'm not perfect either; I slipped up but now I'm better than I've ever been and I know God loves me no matter what. No matter what happens God will always love you. He is real and He is a GREAT GOD.

- Hayden

"Insecurities breed negative thoughts that block your purpose."

DeLana Rutherford

When I tried to be me, I didn't know what to be. .

I fought and I struggled with the inner Me...
I didn't realize it was actually the enemy...
Trying to keep me from what I was destined to be…
I tried to please everyone else, but me...
When I really needed to focus on where I needed to be...
So, I got to a place and really had to see...
Could I be ME, and everyone still love me, totally?
Could I wear my hair like I wanted and embrace the inner me?
Could I sing as loud as I could, even if it was off of key?
See, I had to get to know me, in order to be me, and live life free.
I was tired of pretending that I found me,
Because where I thought I was, was not God's will for me.
Being introduced to the conference changed me greatly.
It helped me release everything I thought I'd be.
It helped me gain what was truly meant for me;
An amazing woman of God full of tranquility.

-Autumn Breeze

"A thankful heart receives much more."

DeLana Rutherford

For 11 years I lived in shame because of my secret past... The past that NO ONE knew about. I was determined that I'd never tell anyone who I used to be and what I used to do. It wasn't until I was 29 years old, had been married for 4 years, and was a mother of two daughters that I shared, with what I felt like the whole world that I used to SELL MY BODY... Yes, I used to be a prostitute and a stripper in my past life. At 16 years old, I went from being a shy and quiet honor roll student to a rebellious teenage runaway. Halfway through my junior year when I should've been picking out a prom dress and studying for exams I was on the streets of Atlanta sleeping with different men to survive.

Eventually I hooked up with a pimp and began working as a stripper as well. At first, I thought that I wanted that seemingly glamorous lifestyle of stripping and making lots of money, but I soon experienced the harsh reality of emptiness, shame and guilt. I'd hurt my parents, dropped out of school a year before graduation, and I had been with so many men, I'd lost count. I hated myself and I felt like a stupid, worthless slut, and felt like I'd never be able to overcome the horrible mess I'd made of my life. Feeling trapped in hopelessness, I ended up sinking deeper into that lifestyle. I began to drink heavily and smoke weed to cope with my pain.

A few days before my 18th birthday, I realized I was tired. After all the long nights, death threats, violent attacks, and various encounters with perverted men, I'd had enough. I decided that I was going to leave that lifestyle for good and try to start all over again. When I told my pimp, they weren't in agreement and their exact words were "if you leave, it's going to be in a body bag, and if you try to run, you're going to get a bullet in your back". So I spent my 18th birthday being held at gunpoint. I was finally able to escape but lived in fear for months afraid that my pimp would track me down and harm me and my family. It was shortly after that I found out about and accepted the amazing love of Jesus and was never the same.

Today, I am thankful for the Be You On Purpose movement because it made me realize that who I am, past, present, and future is valuable to God and His Kingdom. Also, that I never have to hide behind shame again because I'm forever victorious and free in Jesus, my Savior!

-Tequita

"*Every time that you resent who you are, it's an insult to your maker.*"

DeLana Rutherford

Talking about my struggle with weight loss is not easy. The struggle is real. I grew up in a family with great cooks. Love was expressed through cooking and family gatherings. I can remember my middle school and high school days of wanting to participate in sports, but because of the fear of being picked on, I never pursued it. I did branch out and throw shot put and disc my last 4 years in high school. That seemed to be the perfect sport for an overweight person. I have battled with obesity pretty much my whole life.

I have always been a lover of God and one day God redirected my path to a place called Worship with Wonders Church. I had no idea at the time what plans God had for me. Regrets, disappointments, sadness, sorrows and all the things that come with the struggle I had to let go. God placed me in a new place to learn how to "Live a Life of Expectancy". It has always been easy for me to believe God for miracles for other people but when it came to me I had no vision. The manifested miracle of weight loss can seem overwhelming in the eyes of Bethany. In the eyes of God He sees me totally different. My desire is to be in good health. It's not all about being skinny.

My personal journey has not affected my confidence within. Phil 1:6 tells me, "Being confident of this very thing, that He which hath begun a good work in you will perform it until the day of Jesus Christ." God tells me to be confident because it is He that has begun a good work in Bethany. I decided to agree with Him. I am thankful for God filling my life, mouth and mind with new things. In this new place I have learned a lot about myself. I realized that the biggest part of my struggle is quitting. Throughout my weight loss journey I actually saw results but quitting produced more weight gain. It was so easy to go back to the familiar. I allowed the symptoms of the struggle to distract me from the new path God had created for me. Bad reports from the doctor, stress on the job, even worshipping God on the stage. I am still on this journey. I aim to conquer the inner struggle of quitting.

- Bethany

*"Tears cleanse the soul,
let them roll."*

DeLana Rutherford

Christmastime is a time of fun, family and festivity...the phone rang! Time stopped! Life would never be the same!

475 miles and several hours later, we arrived at the hospital in New Orleans. The nurse unzipped the body bag containing my precious son. He had been killed by a careless driver who made a U turn in front of his motorcycle and he plowed into her car. The tornado of emotions struck me all at once − anger, rage, grief, emptiness, vengeance and so many others. This was my beautiful baby boy - his life had just begun. I stroked his forehead for the last time. How could God allow this? We're pastors!

Brad, our youngest son suffered from tics (Tourette's Syndrome) and ADHD, which made school work difficult. To control the tics, the doctor prescribed strong medication...which I believe opened doors to future addiction problems. As a teen, he became addicted to marijuana, Xanax, and other drugs. He began to get in trouble with the law and we got him into diversionary programs and other drug rehabs.......nothing worked! From 14 to 24, our lives were a living hell because we didn't know what Brad would get into. But in 2011, a missionary from Mexico came to minister at our church. I asked Brad to come to the altar and he was miraculously delivered from drugs. The next few months were amazing...he got a great job and was getting his life together. He had fallen in love with Nikki and was making plans to be married. Before they could marry, they found out Nikki was pregnant and Brad was ecstatic! The day of the accident, Brad and Nikki spent the day together. She rode on the back of the motorcycle but Brad made her get off the bike and asked her mother to drive her home. 20 minutes later Brad was gone! Despite the loss and pain, God was in it all! God protected Nikki and the baby (a little boy, Brody who looks just like his daddy); God placed godly people around Brad as he lay in the highway. They prayed for him and God comforted Brad in his last moments on this earth.

As pastors, we can preach the gospel of peace and comfort but can we live it? I decided that I would trust God because He knew everything about the situation and Brad's future choices. I had to thank God for giving me a precious piece of Brad − his son, Brody! I had to decide to FORGIVE the girl who caused the accident and not seek revenge. I had to decide whether or not I truly believed the words of the bible that I preached! I chose to WORSHIP God despite my loss and it drew others to God.

-Sharon

"When you forgive others, you are releasing YOU!"

DeLana Rutherford

*L*ife *seemed good* – on the outside looking in. I had my own law firm, we had nice clothes, a nice house and lived in the right neighborhood. I had two fine stepchildren and my wife and I had adopted a beautiful baby boy and a gorgeous little girl. We were the image of a successful couple, but on the inside, where the world couldn't see, there was a different story. In just 4 ½ years, our marriage – my third, her second – had fallen apart. Marriage counseling wasn't helping. What started out so great had begun to sink as the people we *really* were began to surface.

During this same time, I hired a safety consultant by the name was Bob Borison. On August 24, 1989, Bob came to Bell Law Firm to give a deposition on a case. After that deposition, he and I went to a local restaurant for lunch. While still sitting at the table sipping coffee, Bob looked me in the eye and delivered a message that would change our lives. He said, "Terry, I really don't know you and you don't know me, and I don't really want to do this, but God has given me a message for you." I wasn't anywhere near God at that time, but for some reason, I told him to go ahead. He said, "God said to tell you He wants you back. And so you will know this is from God, He said to tell you He saw you slam your fist on that table and yell at your wife, 'I don't know what you want me to do about it now, I've already made the decision!'".

That statement was word for word from an argument Sharon and I had behind locked doors in our office. NO one was present, and NO one heard – except God. Bob continued: "And further, so you will know this is from Him, He said to tell you, your marriage is falling apart, your finances are crumbling, and your wife is on the verge of suicide." It was all true – and only God could know these things. Bob ended by inviting me to a special service at his church that night. We went to our marriage counselor and told her we weren't coming back, we were getting a divorce, we hated each other. That evening we went to Bob's church. That was Thursday. Sunday, at the evening service in the same church, God filled me with His Spirit. On Wednesday evening He did the same for Sharon. THEN He began to work on us. Now, 25 ½ years later, we have been married 30 years, we are each other's best friend and we pastor a wonderful church.

God saw. He cared. He called. We came. He healed. He repaired. He still sees. He still calls. Will you come?

-Terry

"When we face our enemy, we can find ourselves because it's usually been us all along."

DeLana Rutherford

I struggled with an eating disorder most severely in high school. It became an identity that I took on for myself into college and marriage. In a way, I almost thought that when I walked in a room, people could see it all over me and know my struggles just by looking at me. It was shame that made me believe this lie. I functioned in and out of shame daily. In school, at work, and especially at church, it was exhausting to wear this "outfit" of shame. The more I hid and didn't tell people what I was having a hard time with, the more I thought they KNEW my secret. The more paranoid I was about people finding out, the deeper and darker the secret became. The amount of pretending I thought I had to do was exhausting. NOW, instead of wanting to hide, I want to SHARE my testimony of what I learned about taking care of my body as a precious temple.

I remember hearing that phrase "be you on purpose" for the first time. It hit me so powerfully. I immediately imagined the freedom that would come in that. God showed me that there was freedom in being real. Freedom in exposing what was in the dark. And that it was possible for Him to use this for HIS GOOD.

I love health and the body. It's my PASSION, and I know that God is redeeming the time the enemy stole from me. I believe God had a mark on me to be a powerful influence on others to be healthy, and I also believe the enemy must have seen that early on.

BUT GOD!

PRAISE BE TO GOD for the powerful truth of being myself on PURPOSE. Being who He created me to be. Sharing my struggles on PURPOSE. Shedding light where the enemy would LOVE to keep the darkness.

I went from "Hi, my name is Amy. I have an eating disorder" to "Hi, I am a precious child of the KING, and I am here to help you overcome by the word of my testimony. I am not ashamed of my past. I am proud to be ME."

The enemy TRIED to take me down with the one thing he knew God would use me the most. GOD ALWAYS WINS! FREE TO BE ME!

-Amy

"It's hard to love others when you don't love yourself."

DeLana Rutherford

Growing up in New Orleans and being Catholic was the only thing I knew about religion and church. I went to Catholic school and Mass twice a week. I really had no choice, it was either private school or Catholic schools in Louisiana. When I was 11, I lost my father 3 days before Christmas in a house fire. My life changed. My family moved to Georgia on Christmas Eve 1985, because my Mom had family here and we had nowhere to live. I remember being in a fog for a long time after moving to Georgia. I hated it here – my dad was gone and my friends were all back home in New Orleans. I believe this event changed the course of my life and walk with God.

When I say that I mean I was resentful and fought through many battles as I grew into a young lady. I never felt a desire to know or have a "relationship" with GOD. That grew into a drug addiction, and into fighting and running away from GOD. I fought a crystal meth addiction for 2 years and lost an $80,000 a year job. I had an abusive boyfriend who beat me and later ended up taking his own life. It was a downward spiral. The list could go on.

The day I quit using drugs was the day I found out I was pregnant. In fact, let me tell you how good the grace of GOD really is, in my 8th month I snorted a few lines of crystal meth. Just wanting to get that last high. How selfish right? I had been clean for 8 month, so how did the devil lead me back to the last high. Well, I worried the entire time and felt so much guilt. By the grace of God, my daughter is perfectly healthy and almost 10. She is an honor roll student and in all gifted programs at her school. When they say what the devil uses for harm, God can turn into good, I believe that to be true. By the saving grace of God and His mercy, I'm almost 11 years clean and sober, I have a beautiful daughter who is smart and loves the Lord too.

I now know that my worship and my faith will one day give me eternal life with my father and I rest in knowing all the years I spent wasted mad at God, He made something beautiful from my story. Now it is my turn to teach my daughter not about religion, but about the importance of relationship.

- Heather

"Some people will never celebrate you. They can't value you because they can't even value themselves. They need your prayers more than you need their praise."

DeLana Rutherford

I was 19 years old, a college freshman with dreams, goals, and plans for a successful future. Yet somehow, I was here in the clinic with a positive pregnancy test. I was unprepared for the news and overwhelmed by the thought of life as I knew it being over. I walked out of that clinic to go take my final exams with one goal in mind – to abort. I wept for the death of a child I would never meet. People's morals and values would not raise a child. The father and I were in agreement; we were not ready. I immediately scheduled the abortion. I cried, relentlessly. There was a war in my mind between keep it and kill it, until one night, as I lay in my bed, with a wet face, I had an ear to hear His voice. It was so new to me and still so comforting. The Lord spoke, "Your child's purpose is far greater than your goals".

He saved two lives that night. I was a single, pregnant teenager facing the humiliation alone, except, I wasn't alone at all. I felt His presence when I cried, when I doubted, when I feared. His arms wrapped me tightly at night when I couldn't bare the pain any longer. He graced me. Physically, pregnancy was easy, but emotionally, it was the hardest thing I ever faced. In hindsight, I know it was because a war for two lives had been won, and the purification process had ensued. He stripped me. He stripped me to my core. I was naked, and it hurt to the deepest parts of my soul. But I was loved, I was comforted, and I was known. He had to take away all the things and people that would hinder His work. A queen was coming and she would receive a royal welcome from a mother that had been made clean by the King. He surrounded me with His presence, His angels, and His people. Like pieces to a puzzle, He connected me to Worship with Wonders Church, a spiritual family and faith filled friends. And so it was, at the tender age of 19, the Lord brought forth the harvest He had been preparing in me. Two servants with One Master.

-Kayla

"be YOU on purpose!"

DeLana Rutherford

My prayer is that each one of these stories has touched your life in some way.

My purpose for writing this book was not to celebrate the pain that so many went through, but to celebrate their victory and choice to overcome in the midst of what seemed impossible.

Thank you for taking time to read each story. I trust that you have been encouraged to tell your story and be YOU on purpose.

If you would like more information on the be YOU on purpose movement, donate to the purpose or share your story with us, please visit www.MylesandDeLana.com